612
E

Elgin

The human bod

DATE DUE

FEB 2

OCT 2

MAY

NOV 1

DEC

612
E

Elgin

The human body: the muscles

DATE DUE	BORROWER'S NAME	ROOM NUMBER
FEB 2	Hinsen 12/70	T
OCT 2 8	Jenny	25
MAY 8		
NOV		

DEMCO

THE HUMAN BODY:
The Muscles

THE HUMAN BODY:
The Muscles

Written and illustrated
by Kathleen Elgin

FRANKLIN WATTS, INC.
New York, 1973

612
E

Library of Congress Cataloging in Publication Data

Elgin, Kathleen.
  The human body.

  SUMMARY: Describes the various types of muscles – skeletal, smooth, and cardiac – and how they
function.
  1. Muscles – Juvenile literature. [1. Muscles]
I. Title.
QP301.E56   612′.74   72-8130
ISBN 0-531-01181-X

THE HUMAN BODY:
The Muscles

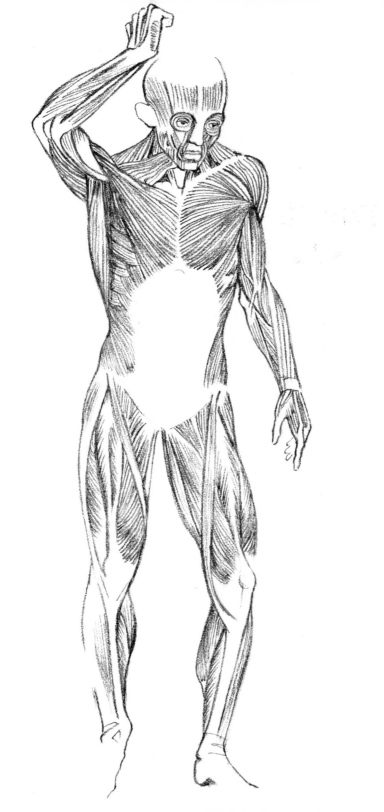

If it were not for your muscles, nothing in
   your body could move. You could not
   swallow, blink an eye, or breathe. You
   could not digest your food. You could not
   lift your arm or take a step. Your heart
   could not beat. Blood could not circulate
   throughout your body.
Muscles make all these actions possible.
   Every time any part of you moves, your
   muscles are working. They are the movers
   of your body.

There are three different types of muscle: *skeletal, smooth,* and *cardiac.*

Skeletal muscles are attached to the bones of your skeleton. They move the bones.

Smooth muscle is found inside your body, in the walls of your stomach, intestines, glands, and other organs. Smooth muscle is also found in your blood vessels and skin.

Cardiac muscle is found *only* in the walls of your heart — nowhere else. "Cardiac" comes from a Greek word meaning "heart."

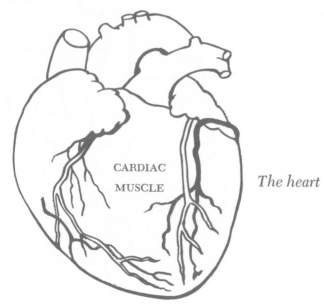

CARDIAC
MUSCLE

The heart

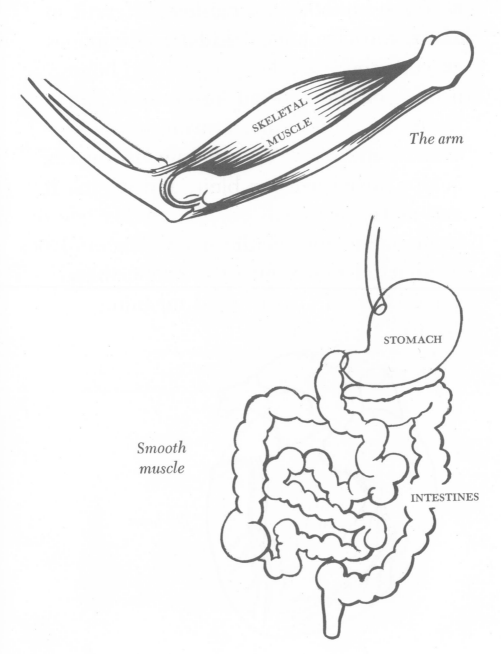

SKELETAL MUSCLE

The arm

STOMACH

Smooth muscle

INTESTINES

9

The three kinds of muscle are different in some ways, but they do have things in common.

All muscles can shorten, or *contract*. By shortening, they make various parts of your body move. To see how this works, take a strong rubber band and stretch it out as far as it will go. Then relax one of your hands and let the band shorten. Does your hand move with the rubber band?

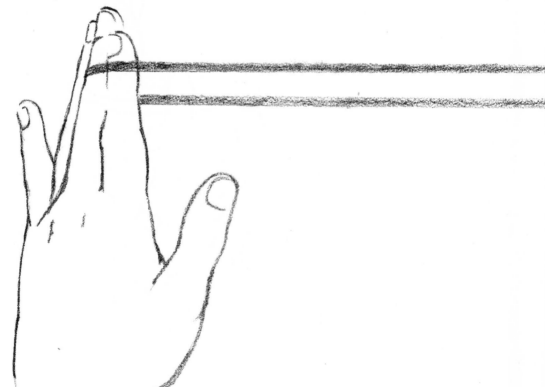

Muscles work in the same way as the rubber band. When the muscles contract, they move the parts of the body to which they are fastened.

When more movement is needed, the muscles contract more. When less movement is needed, they contract less.

All muscles can stretch when heavy force is put on them. But they are elastic and go back to their former shape when the force becomes less.

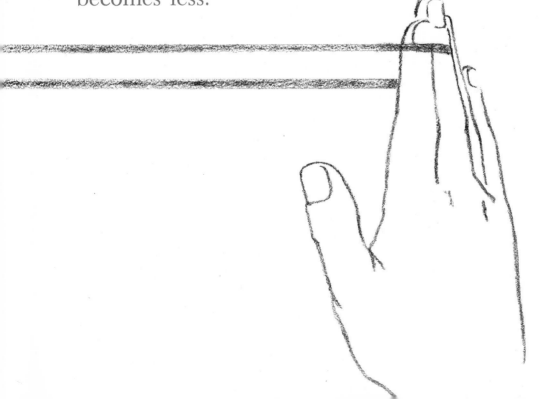

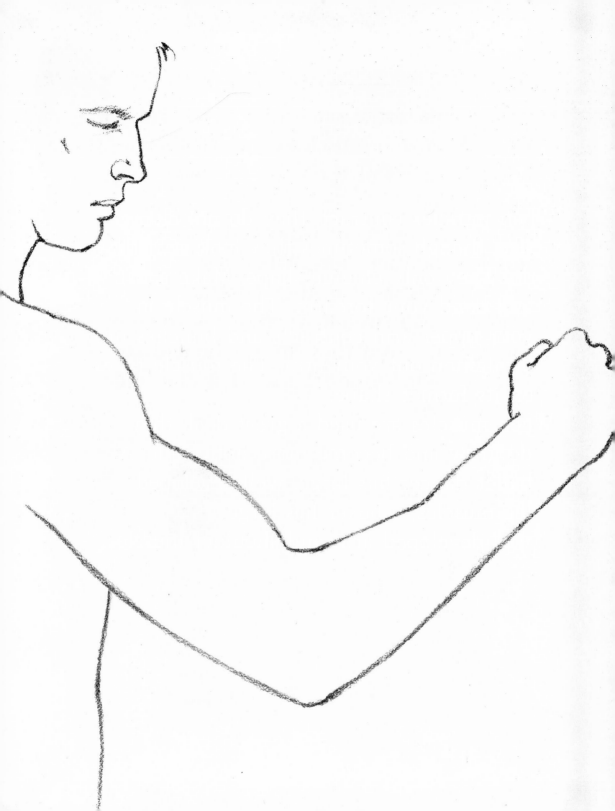

When muscles contract, they do not change size, though sometimes they look as if they do. They only change shape. Make a fist and bend your forearm. The muscle in your upper arm contracts and bunches up. Straighten out your arm. The muscle takes on its former shape.

When muscles are used a great deal, they do grow and become more noticeable. A ballet dancer has large, well-developed leg muscles; a boxer has large, well-developed arm and shoulder muscles.

All muscles have nerves that carry messages to and from your central nervous system — your brain and spinal cord. As things happen around you, *afferent* nerves are constantly sending messages *from* the muscles to the central nervous system. Then answering messages run along *efferent* nerves from the central nervous system *to* the muscles. The muscles contract or relax according to the message sent. These messages direct the movement of your muscles. The information they give is necessary in helping you to keep your balance and in making all your muscular movements work together, or *coordinate*.

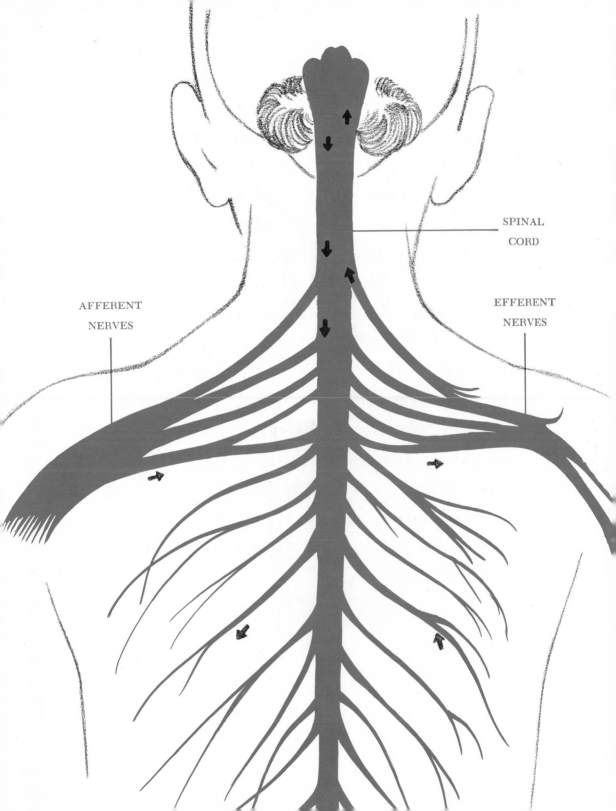

SPINAL
CORD

AFFERENT
NERVES

EFFERENT
NERVES

Some of your muscles, such as the skeletal
muscles, work in response to a thought in
your brain — in response to your will.
(Your brain is directing the movement
when you kick a ball, for instance.) The
muscles directed in this way are called
voluntary muscles. "Voluntary" comes
from a Latin word meaning "will."

Some of your muscles, like the cardiac
muscle, work without any thought on
your part — without your will. These are
called *involuntary* muscles. The smooth
muscles — in your stomach, your intestines,
and other organs — are involuntary
muscles.

If nerve messages from the brain fail to
reach the skeletal muscles because of some
injury to the nerves, the muscles cannot
move. They have become *paralyzed.*

Your muscles stay a little contracted, a
little tense, all the time. This tenseness is
called muscle *tone*, and it keeps the
muscles ready to respond to a nerve
message.

Your skeletal muscles are arranged in the
body so that they are held in a slight
stretch over the joints. If your leg muscles,
for instance, were entirely relaxed, your
legs would buckle and you would fall in
a heap. If you have ever been ill in bed
for a long time, you know how wobbly
you are when you start to walk. Your
muscles have lost their tone. With exercise,
they will get it back.

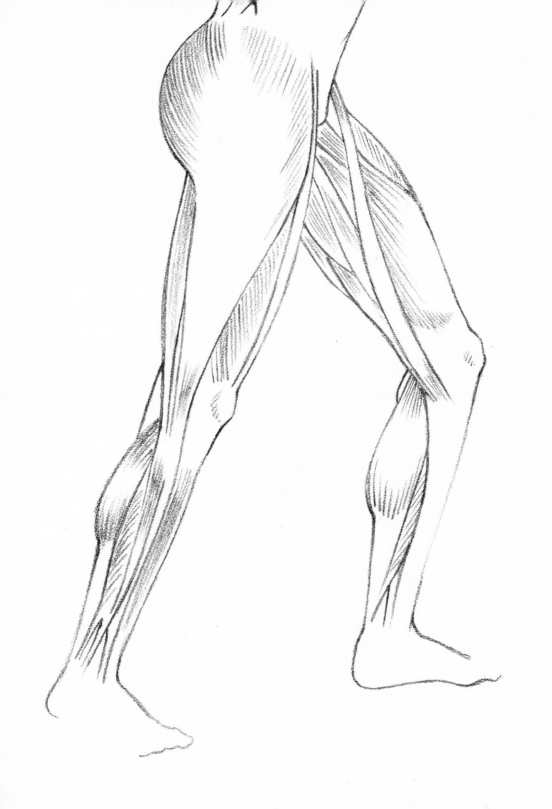

To do their work, muscles need fuel — the food you eat. Muscles produce heat while they are working. This heat is a chief means of keeping your body at its proper temperature. In hot weather you take it easy and do not use your muscles as much. In cold weather you move around rapidly to make body heat. If you cannot do this, you may start to shiver — an involuntary way of moving your muscles and increasing heat production.

Your heat production does not stop when you go to bed at night. While you are asleep, some heat is made by the activity of the muscles that you use in breathing, by the heart muscle, and by the smooth muscles in the walls of the blood vessels and various organs.

The heart — the cardiac muscle — is a hollow
and somewhat cone-shaped muscle. As its
walls contract and relax they pump blood
throughout the body. This steady motion
makes the heartbeat that can be heard
in the chest.

The heart muscle never stops working
during a lifetime. It contracts at a rate of
70 to 75 times a minute, and each day it
pumps over 3,000 gallons of blood. The
blood continually circulates throughout
the body and comes back to the heart to
be pumped again.

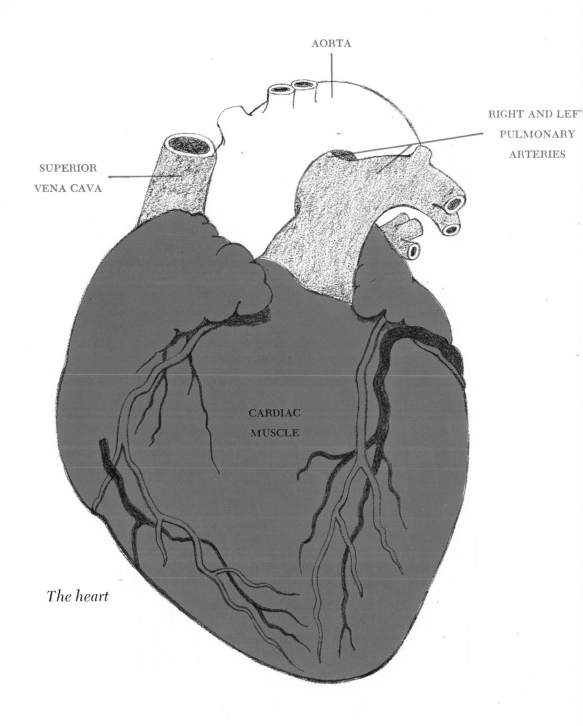

AORTA

RIGHT AND LEF[T]
PULMONARY
ARTERIES

SUPERIOR
VENA CAVA

CARDIAC
MUSCLE

The heart

Muscle is made of *tissue*. Tissue is living material composed of tiny units called *cells*. The cells of cardiac muscle are roughly four-sided. These cells are arranged in such a way that they form branching fibers. The fibers stretch easily to make the heart larger when it receives blood from the body and they contract strongly to force the blood on its way again.

CARDIAC MUSCLE FIBERS
(GREATLY ENLARGED)

The cells of smooth muscles are arranged in layers that form very strong, thin, smooth sheets. Smooth muscles can stretch a great deal, if necessary, and they change shape to accommodate their tasks. Your stomach, for instance, stretches to hold a big meal, and it contracts when it is empty.

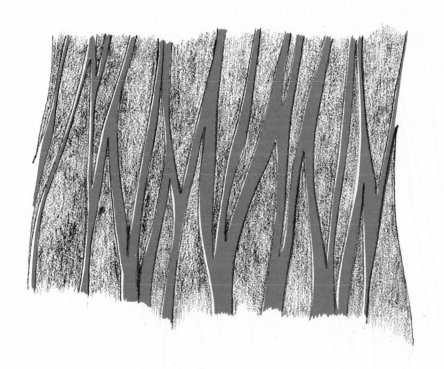

SMOOTH MUSCLE SECTION
(GREATLY ENLARGED)

Skeletal-muscle cells are long and thin, like fibers, and are divided crosswise into many little bundles. The longer the fibers, the greater is the muscle's range of movement. The greater the number of fibers, the greater the muscle's strength. Because skeletal muscles have crosswise light and dark sections, they are often called *striated*, or striped, muscles.

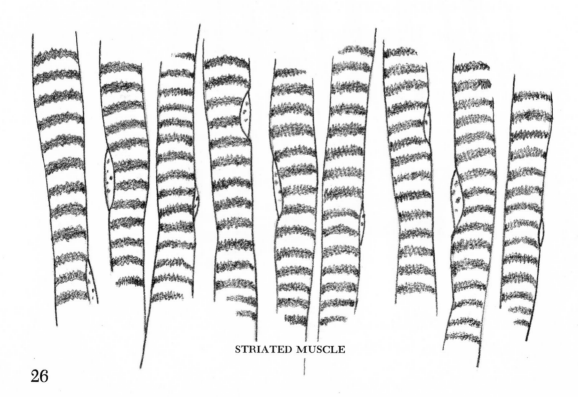

STRIATED MUSCLE

Skeletal muscles are fastened to their
anchoring points by a different kind of
tissue. Most skeletal muscles are fastened
by tissues called *tendons*. You can see
tendons moving under the skin on the
back of your hand as you open and
close it.

Tendons vary in shape according to the
muscle they serve. Some tendons are like
white cords, some are like flat sheets, and
some are like ribbons. They are all very
strong, as they have to stand up under
great force.

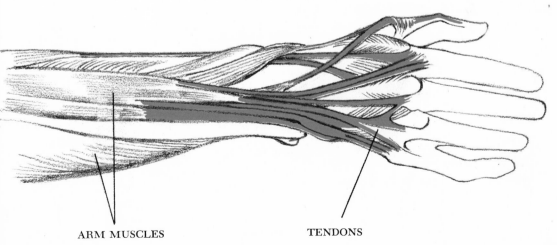

ARM MUSCLES   TENDONS

No bone can move by itself. Skeletal muscles
have to move the bones, but they can do
this only at the *joints*. When a bone moves,
its muscle has shortened and has pulled
on a tendon, which is firmly anchored.
This pull forces the bone to change
position at a joint.

Each skeletal muscle is fixed more firmly at
one end than at another. The more firmly
fixed end is called the muscle's *origin*. The
other end of the muscle is usually attached
to the part that is movable. This end is
called the *insertion.*
The ability of a muscle to contract, or
shorten, toward its point of origin makes
motion possible. Some muscles also can
pull first toward one of their ends, then
toward the other end.

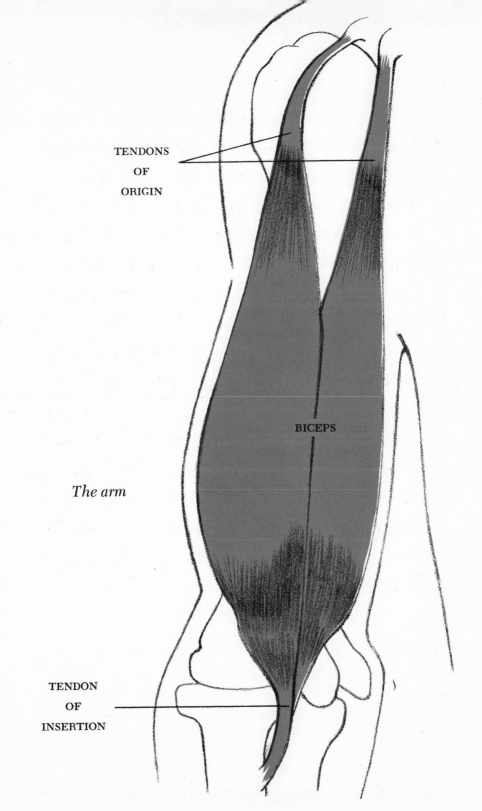

TENDONS
OF
ORIGIN

BICEPS

The arm

TENDON
OF
INSERTION

Muscles cannot push; they can only pull. When a muscle has done its work, it relaxes and stops pulling. Some muscles work in opposing pairs, to move bones in opposite directions at different times. When one of these muscles contracts, the other relaxes. For example, when you bend your forearm, the muscle called the *biceps* contracts and pulls the arm up. The muscle behind the biceps — the *triceps* — is relaxed. But when you extend your forearm, the biceps relaxes and the triceps contracts, making your forearm unbend. In most cases, many different muscles work together to make any movement possible.

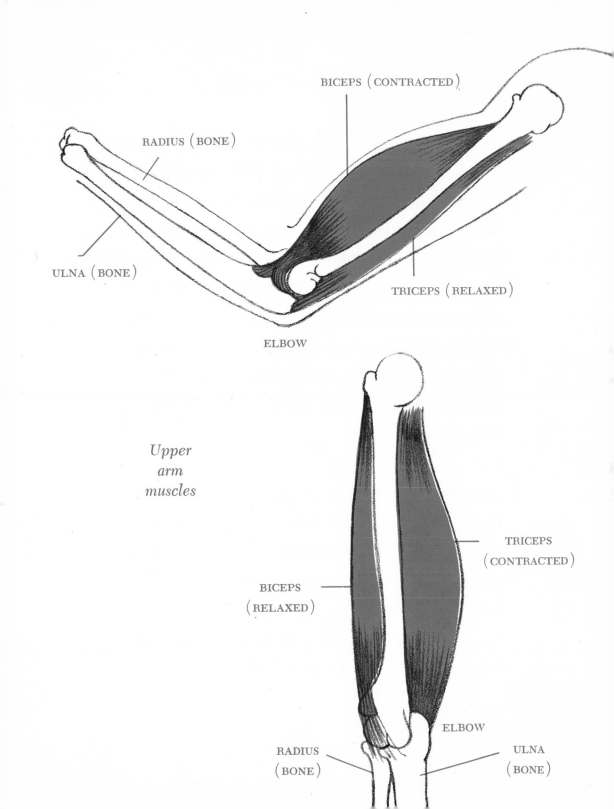

BICEPS (CONTRACTED)

RADIUS (BONE)

ULNA (BONE)

TRICEPS (RELAXED)

ELBOW

Upper arm muscles

TRICEPS (CONTRACTED)

BICEPS (RELAXED)

ELBOW

RADIUS (BONE)

ULNA (BONE)

Muscles have a great variety of shapes and sizes. They are formed differently according to the job they have to do. Some muscles move the bones; others move body organs or parts of them. Some muscles are quite large and powerful; some are small and have little strength. Muscles are named for their size, shape, placement, structure, direction of movement, action, or the way they are attached.

For example, the *deltoid*, the shoulder muscle, is shaped like the Greek letter *delta*, or △. And the *biceps*, one of the arm muscles, gets its name because it has two heads, or origins. (*Bi* means "two" and *ceps* means "head," in Latin; the whole word means "two-headed.")

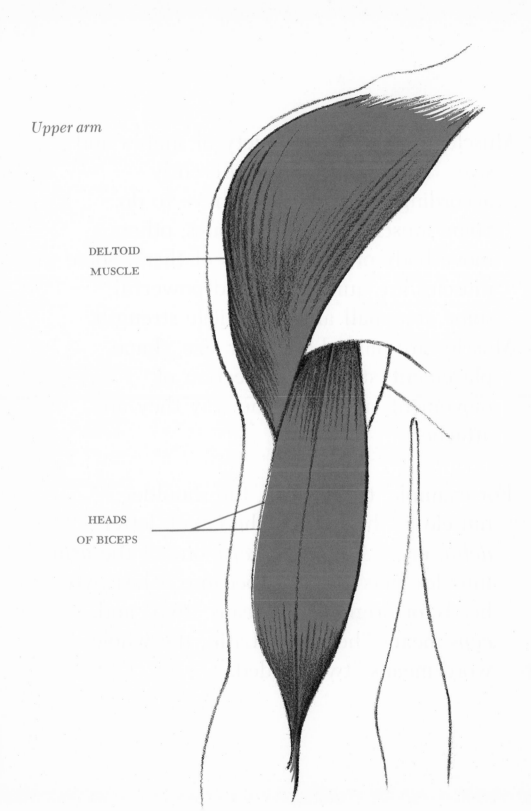

Upper arm

DELTOID
MUSCLE

HEADS
OF BICEPS

A large number of your muscles — over six
hundred of them — are skeletal muscles.
And one-fourth of all your muscles are
in your face and neck.

The facial muscles are small and thin. They
attach to the skin as well as to the bones.
Some are less than an inch long.

They can raise an eyebrow.

They can cause a frown.

They can make a smile or a grin.

They are very special muscles. You cannot,
for instance, change the expression of the
skin on your arm or chest, but you can
on your face.

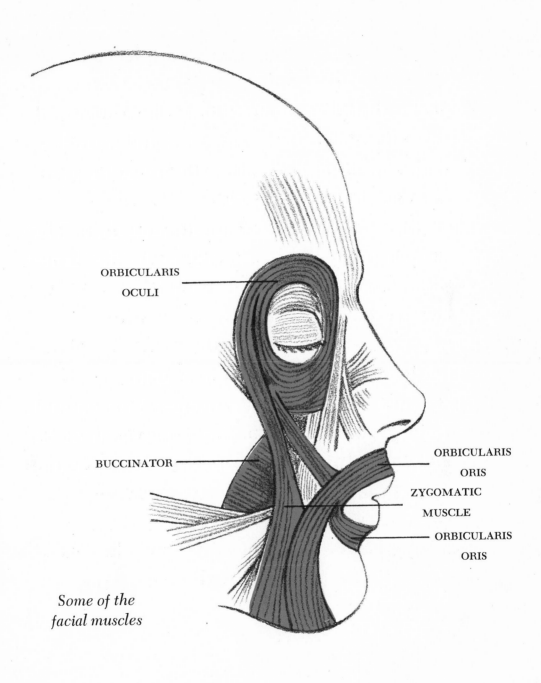

ORBICULARIS
OCULI

BUCCINATOR

ORBICULARIS
ORIS

ZYGOMATIC
MUSCLE

ORBICULARIS
ORIS

*Some of the
facial muscles*

The *orbicularis oculi* (or-BIK-yoo-LAH-ris OK-yoo-lie) acts as a shield, guarding each eye against injury.

The *buccinator* (BUK-sin-AY-tor) keeps the cheek close to the teeth. This muscle, working together with some other facial muscles, and the tongue helps make it possible for food to be ground between the teeth. It also helps in whistling or blowing musical wind instruments. One of the buccinator muscles lies on each side of the face.

The *orbicularis oris* (or-BIK-yoo-LAH-ris OH-ris) and its helpers move the lips for speaking, eating, and all the various expressions of the mouth.

The *zygomatic* (ZY-go-MAT-ik) muscle raises each corner of the mouth when you smile or laugh.

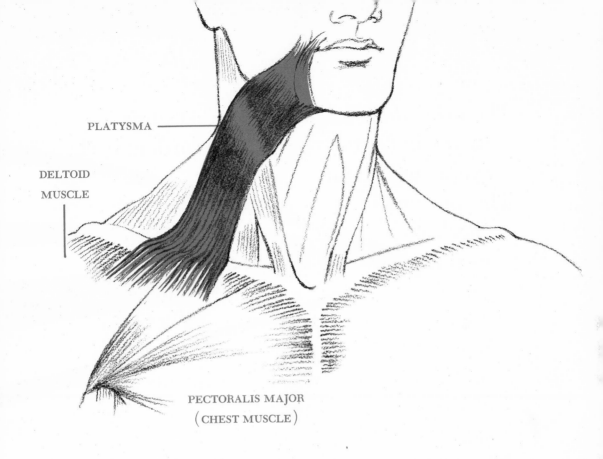

PLATYSMA

DELTOID
MUSCLE

PECTORALIS MAJOR
(CHEST MUSCLE)

The *platysma* (pla-TIZ-ma) is a broad sheet of muscle that lies just under the skin, in the front and on each side of the neck. It wrinkles the skin of the neck, lowers the corners of the mouth, and makes expressions of sadness and of fear.

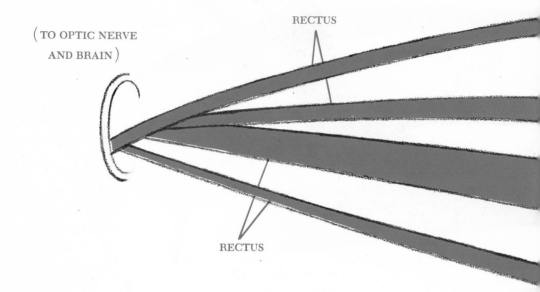

The eye and its muscles
(greatly enlarged)

RECTUS

(TO OPTIC NERVE
AND BRAIN)

RECTUS

Six muscles control the movement of each
eyeball. They make it possible for you to
glance in various directions without
moving your head. There are four *rectus*
(REK-tus) muscles and two *oblique* (ob-LEEK)
muscles in each eye. These muscles are
highly coordinated. The muscles of the
two eyeballs work together.

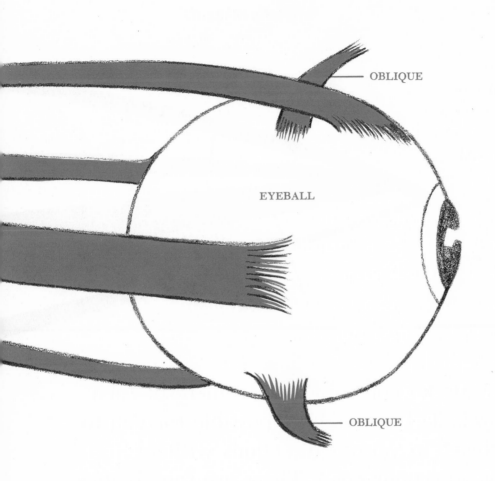

OBLIQUE

EYEBALL

OBLIQUE

The chewing and swallowing of food are
made possible by the coordinated action
of many muscles, including that voluntary
muscle, the *tongue*.

The tongue is a bundle of various muscles.
A V-shaped groove on its upper surface
divides it into two parts. The forward
part is called the *dorsum*. The rear part
is called the *root*. Five muscles entering
the tongue from outside itself serve to
move it in any direction desired. Other
muscles wholly within the tongue help it
change shape and position in eating,
tasting, swallowing, and speaking.

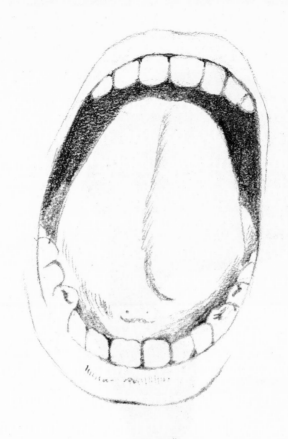

*Open mouth,
showing tongue
behind teeth*

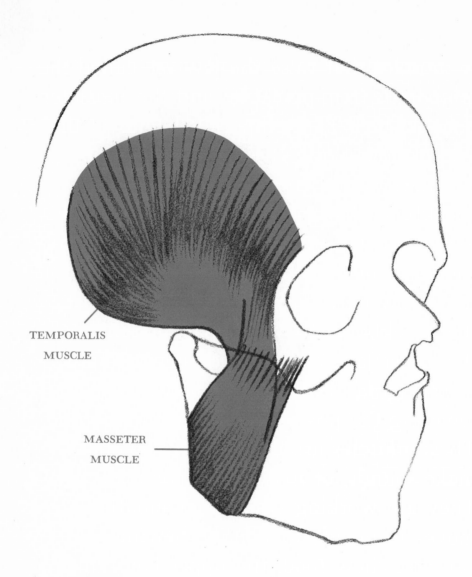

TEMPORALIS
MUSCLE

MASSETER
MUSCLE

PTERYGOID MUSCLES

The muscles that raise the jaw are called the *temporalis* (tem-po-RAL-is) and the *masseter* (mas-SEE-ter). The temporalis begins at the side of your skull. It is wide at the top and narrows down as it fits under the cheekbone. Its very end is inserted in the lower jaw. One temporalis muscle lies on each side of your face.

The narrow part of the masseter begins at the cheekbone. Its wider part attaches to the lower jaw, on each side of your face.

The *pterygoid* (TER-y-goid) muscles help in lowering the jaw and opening the mouth. These muscles are used when you speak, make sounds, or make room for food. They are working when your mouth moves from side to side in chewing.

When you chew food, the upper jaw remains motionless. The lower jaw does all the work. That is why you have strong muscles to raise the lower jaw.

Two important sets of muscles in your neck move your head from side to side and up and down. These are the *sternocleidomastoid* (STER-no-KLI-do-MAS-toid) muscles and the *splenius* (SPLEE-nee-us) muscles.

The sternocleidomastoids look like two rubber hoses that bulge in the center. These muscles run down each side of the neck. They begin at the base of the skull behind the ears, and attach to the collarbones.

The flat splenius muscles begin in the back and neck, and attach to the base of the skull behind the ears.

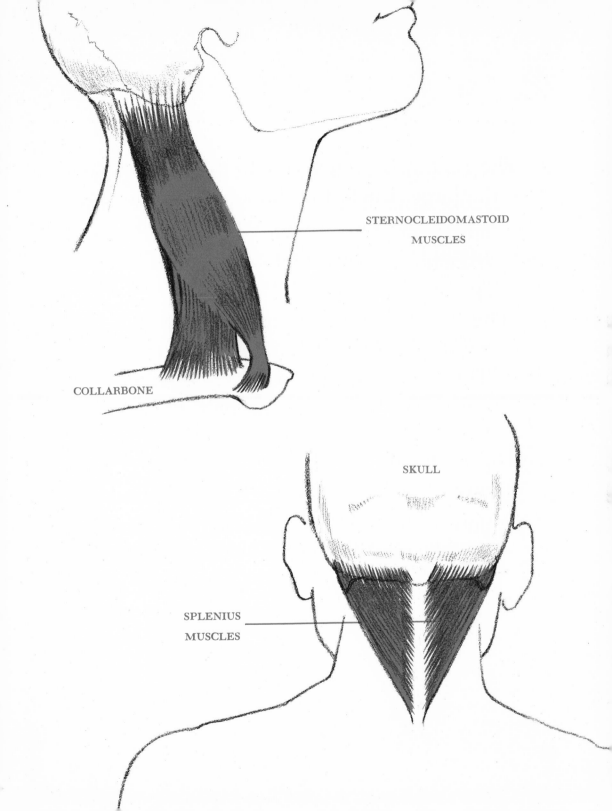

STERNOCLEIDOMASTOID
MUSCLES

COLLARBONE

SKULL

SPLENIUS
MUSCLES

The *pectoralis major* (PEK-to-RAL-is MA-jor) is
the large, thick, fan-shaped chest muscle.
It is made up of many flat bands. They
spread from the collarbone down the
outside of the breastbone and across your
seventh rib. The outer ends of these
muscular bands twist upon themselves and
fit into the top inner side of the upper
arm. There is one set of these muscles on
each side of the chest.

The *pectoralis minor* is a thin, triangular
muscle that lies under the pectoralis
major. This muscle helps move the
shoulder and the upper arm. There is one
on each side of the chest.

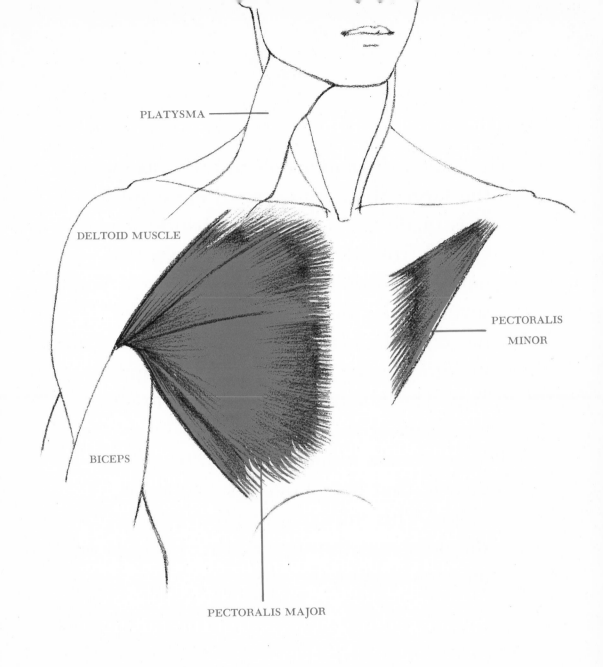

PLATYSMA

DELTOID MUSCLE

PECTORALIS
MINOR

BICEPS

PECTORALIS MAJOR

The muscles of the shoulder and the back are powerful flat bands that help control the movement of neck, back, and arms.

The most important of these muscles are the *trapezius* (tra-PEE-zee-us), the *teres* (tir-EEZ) *major*, the *teres minor*, the *deltoid* (DEL-toid), and the *latissimus dorsi* (lat-ISS-i-mus DOR-sie).

The trapezius begins at the base of the skull and ends at the vertebra in the middle of the back. It extends to the collarbone and to the shoulder blade on each side of the body. It lifts and moves the shoulder blade.

The teres major and teres minor are thick muscles that help extend and move the arms. The deltoid muscles are thick, coarse muscles also. They control the raising and lowering of the arms.

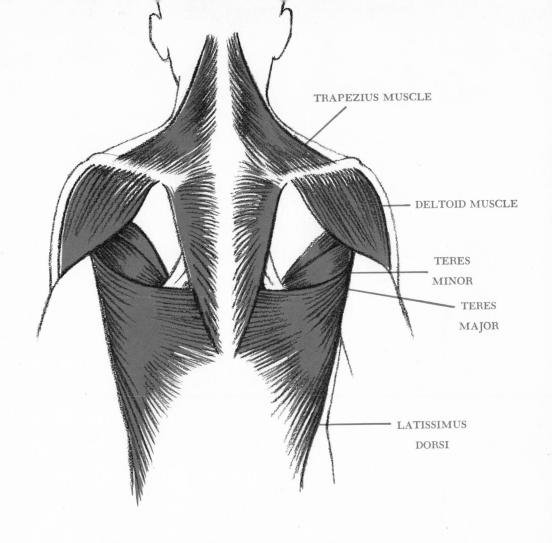

TRAPEZIUS MUSCLE

DELTOID MUSCLE

TERES
MINOR

TERES
MAJOR

LATISSIMUS
DORSI

The latissimus dorsi muscles pull the arms down, turn them inward, and also pull them behind the back.

The muscles of the ribs are called the *intercostals* (IN-ter-COST-als). They raise and lower the rib cage, which contains the lungs. By their action they make it possible for you to breathe. One set of intercostal muscles raises the rib cage by pulling the ribs up and outward. The other set of muscles lowers the rib cage by pulling the ribs down.

When the ribs are raised, the lungs expand into the larger space that has been made, so that they have a larger capacity. Air is breathed in. When the first set of muscles, which pulls the ribs up, relaxes, the second set of muscles pulls the ribs down, closer together. The lungs have less capacity, and air is breathed out.

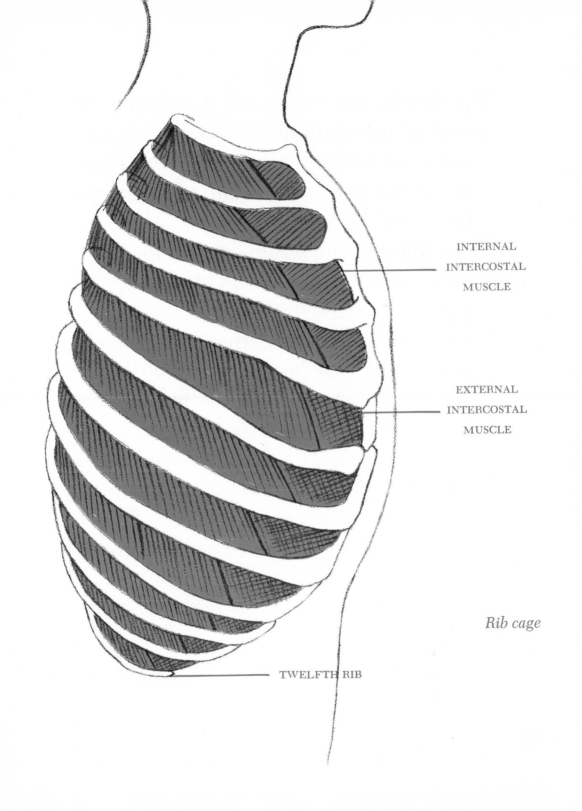

INTERNAL
INTERCOSTAL
MUSCLE

EXTERNAL
INTERCOSTAL
MUSCLE

Rib cage

TWELFTH RIB

The *diaphragm* (DI-a-fram) is a strong, thin wall of muscle that divides the rib cage from the abdominal cavity. The upper surface of the diaphragm helps support the heart and lungs.

When you breathe in, or *inhale*, the diaphragm moves downward to make more room in the rib cage.

When you breathe out, or *exhale*, the diaphragm muscle relaxes upward to make the size of the rib cage smaller.

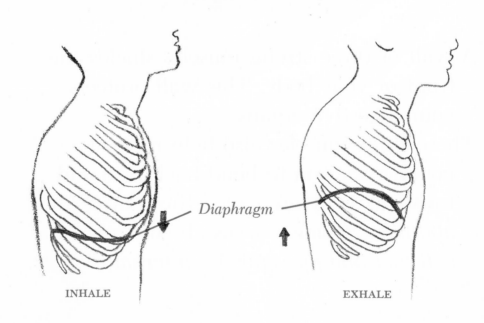

Diaphragm

INHALE   EXHALE

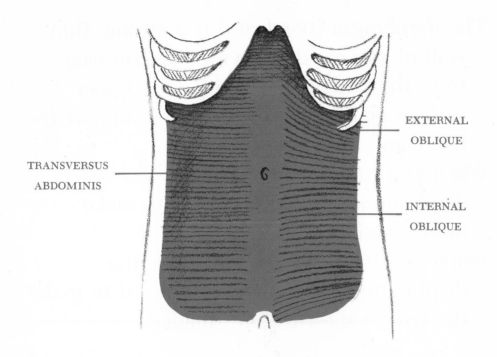

TRANSVERSUS
ABDOMINIS

EXTERNAL
OBLIQUE

INTERNAL
OBLIQUE

A wall of three strong muscles shields the
front of your body. This wall protects
your digestive organs.

These three muscles also help make it
possible for you to bend backward and
forward. They are called the *transversus
abdominis* (trans-VER-sus ab-DOM-i-nis), the
external oblique, and the *internal oblique*.

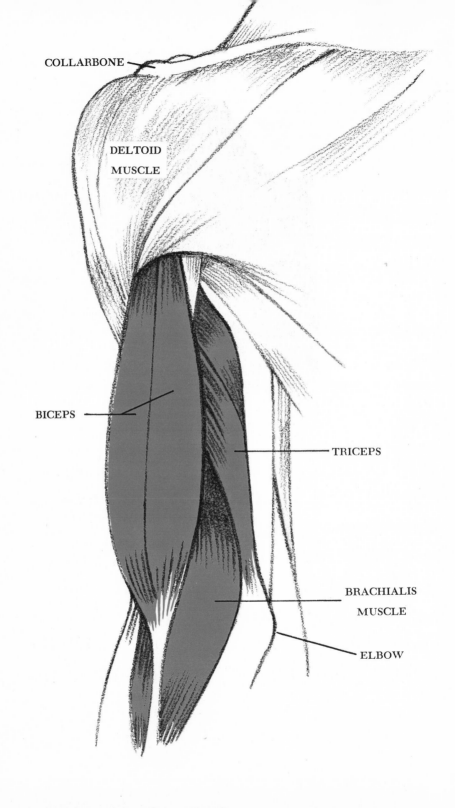

COLLARBONE

DELTOID
MUSCLE

BICEPS

TRICEPS

BRACHIALIS
MUSCLE

ELBOW

The important muscles of the upper arm are
long and wiry. They are called the *triceps*
(TRI-seps), the *biceps* (BI-seps), and the
brachialis (BRACK-ee-AL-is).
The triceps works with the biceps in
bending the elbow and controlling the
movement of the forearm.
The brachialis is also a powerful mover of
the forearm.

The important muscles of the forearm are
the *brachioradialis* (BRACK-ee-o-RAY-dee-AL-is),
the *supinator* (SOO-pin-AY-tor), and the
pronator teres (PRO-NAY-tor tir-EEZ).

The brachioradialis, a long tough muscle,
begins at the elbow and stretches to the
outside of the wrist.

The supinator is a broad sheet of muscle
that begins in the upper arm bone. It
wraps around to end in the *radius*, one of
the two bones of the forearm. It rotates
the arm so that the palm of the hand is
toward the front.

The pronator begins at the elbow and ends
at the *ulna*, the other bone of the lower
arm. It rotates the arm so that the palm
of the hand is toward the back.

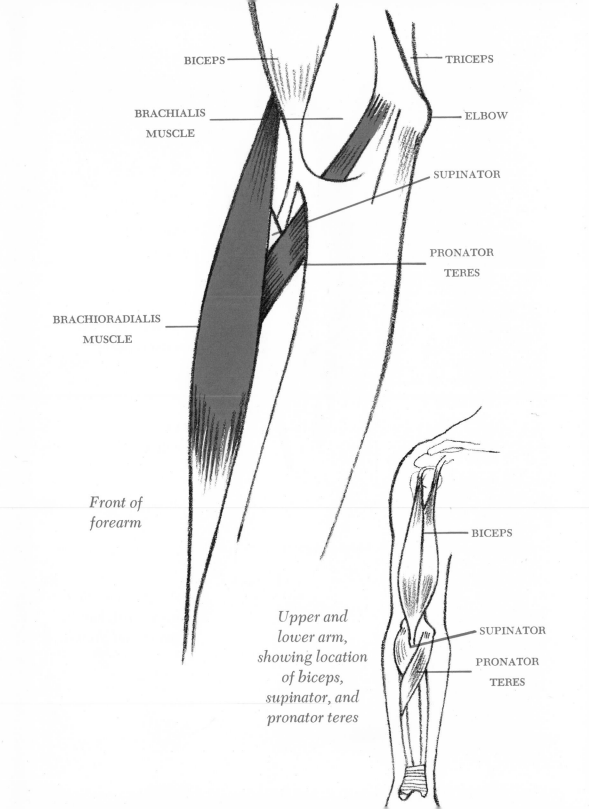

BICEPS

TRICEPS

BRACHIALIS
MUSCLE

ELBOW

SUPINATOR

PRONATOR
TERES

BRACHIORADIALIS
MUSCLE

*Front of
forearm*

BICEPS

SUPINATOR

PRONATOR
TERES

*Upper and
lower arm,
showing location
of biceps,
supinator, and
pronator teres*

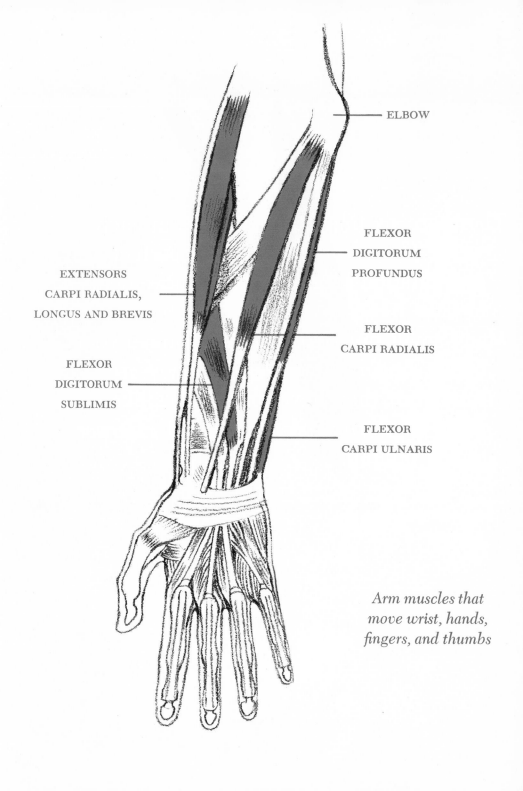

ELBOW

FLEXOR
DIGITORUM
PROFUNDUS

EXTENSORS
CARPI RADIALIS,
LONGUS AND BREVIS

FLEXOR
CARPI RADIALIS

FLEXOR
DIGITORUM
SUBLIMIS

FLEXOR
CARPI ULNARIS

*Arm muscles that
move wrist, hands,
fingers, and thumbs*

There are six important muscles in each wrist. They work together in perfect coordination to give flexible movement to your hands.

Many small but strong muscles move your hands, fingers, and thumbs. They are small, but they have long names like *flexor digitorum profundus* and *extensor digitis minimi*.

The muscles of the lower rear part of the trunk are three: the *gluteus maximus* (GLOO-tee-us MAX-i-mus), the *gluteus medius* (MEE-dee-us), and the *gluteus minimus* (MIN-i-mus).

They contract to move the hip joints in the actions of running, climbing, and going upstairs. They also help to raise the body from a stooping or sitting position.

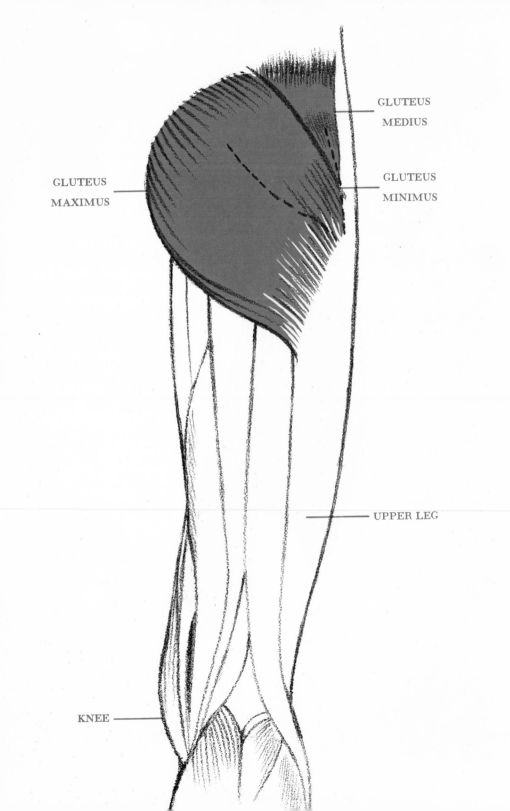

GLUTEUS
MEDIUS

GLUTEUS
MAXIMUS

GLUTEUS
MINIMUS

UPPER LEG

KNEE

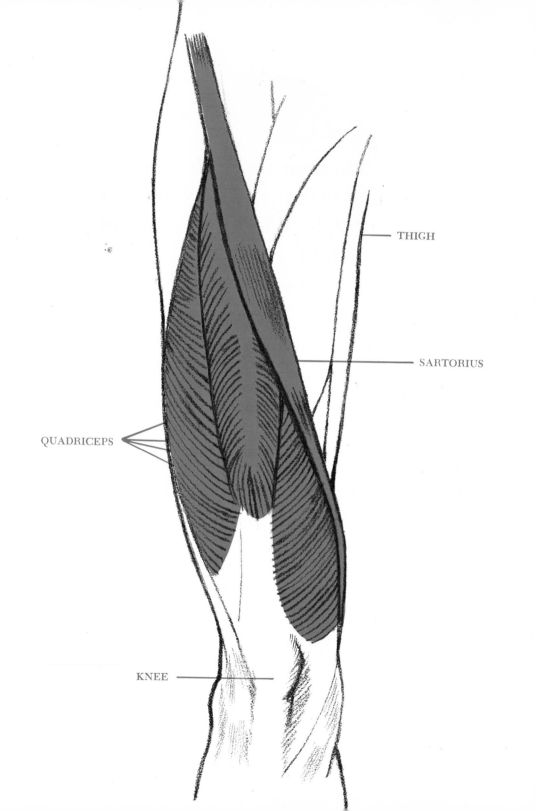

THIGH

SARTORIUS

QUADRICEPS

KNEE

These muscles maintain the body's balance
in the action of walking and running. The
muscles of the right side contract to tilt
the hips to the right as the left leg leaves
the ground and moves forward.

The longest muscle in the body is in the
thigh. It is called the *sartorius*
(sar-TO-ree-us), from the Latin word for
tailor. This muscle, one in each thigh,
allows you to sit cross-legged, the
traditional position of the tailor.

The sartorius and four bundles of muscles
called the *quadriceps* (KWOD-ri-seps) help
you keep your balance as well as move
your legs.

The important muscles in the lower leg
are the *soleus* (SO-lee-us) and the
gastrocnemius (GAS-tro-NEE-mee-us).
The soleus and the gastrocnemius are the
calf muscles. They raise your heel from
the ground and keep you balanced for
action. These two muscles are the main
driving forces in walking, running,
dancing, and jumping.

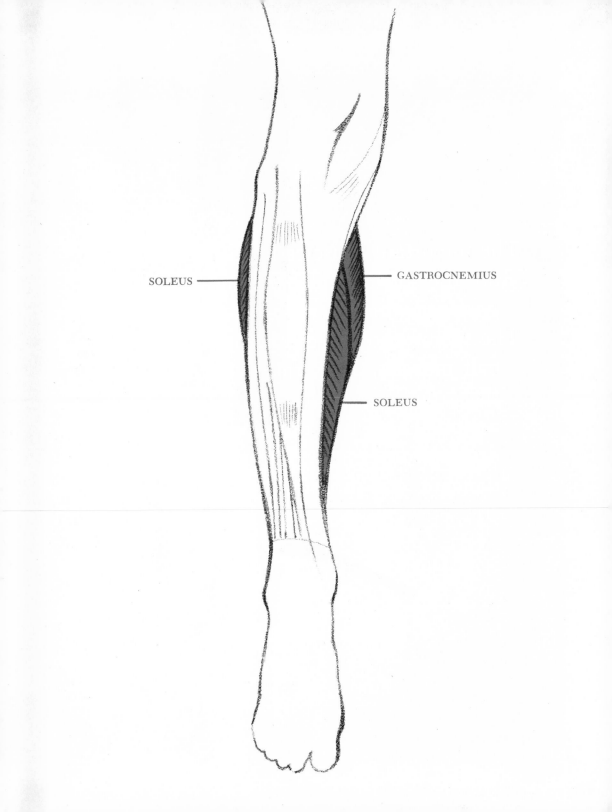

SOLEUS

GASTROCNEMIUS

SOLEUS

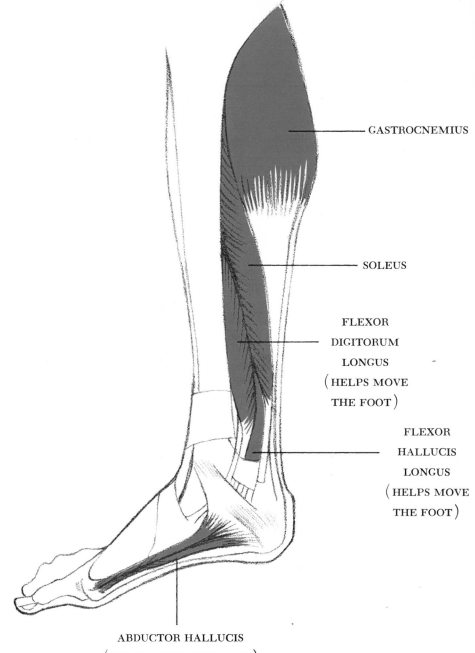

GASTROCNEMIUS

SOLEUS

FLEXOR
DIGITORUM
LONGUS
(HELPS MOVE
THE FOOT)

FLEXOR
HALLUCIS
LONGUS
(HELPS MOVE
THE FOOT)

ABDUCTOR HALLUCIS
(HELPS MOVE THE FOOT)

The human foot is unusual because, unlike other animal feet, it is arched. It is fashioned to support an upright body. The arch enables you to take a gentle walk or make a six-foot jump while it absorbs the jarring shocks that might run up your spine, without it.

Muscles support the bones of the arch, which is designed to distribute your body weight throughout the foot. The arch provides the strength and firm structure so that the foot can be used as a lever, to push you forward when you walk.

The small muscles of the foot help you keep your balance and they aid the muscles of the leg in running, stretching, and bending. When you walk or take just one step, about three hundred muscles of your body are in motion.

Every muscle of your body is designed to
fit a particular need. Many sets of skeletal
muscles — some contracting, some relaxing
— help the body move and balance in
every position. The system of bones and
muscles works together beautifully. And
the many unseen smooth muscles and the
heart muscle perform their work quietly
and unceasingly, day after day, year
after year.

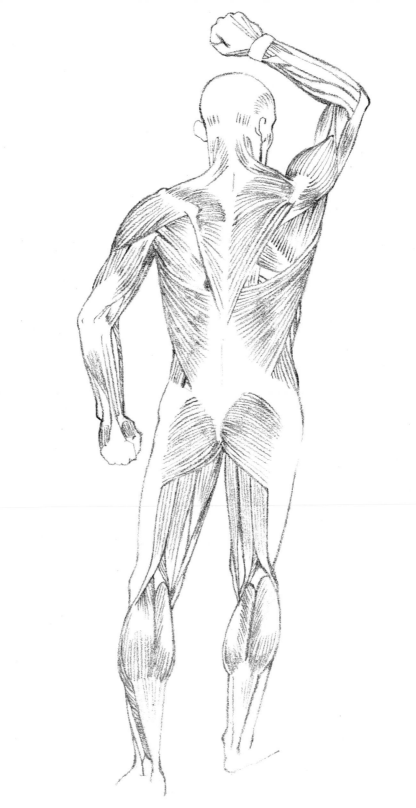

INDEX

ABOUT THE AUTHOR

Kathleen Elgin attended the Dayton (Ohio) Art Institute, and the American School of Design. She has done free-lance work in advertising and has illustrated many books for young people, including the "Human Body" series, which she has both written and illustrated. In 1969, at the Children's Book Fair in Bologna, Italy, an international jury awarded a Graphic Prize for Children's Books to Miss Elgin for *The Heart*, a title in the "Human Body" series. She makes her home in New York City and on Fire Island, New York.